Introduction to Open and Relational Theology

Introduction to
Open and Relational Theology

under the supervision of
Thomas Jay Oord

Theological Essentials

©Digital Theological Library 2025

Library of Congress Cataloging-in-Publication Data

Thomas Jay Oord (creator).
Introduction to Open and Relational Theology/
Thomas Jay Oord
97 + x pp. cm. 12.7 x 20.32
ISBN 979-8-89731-078-4 (Print)
ISBN 979-8-89731-079-1 (Ebook)
ISBN 979-8-89731-080-7 (Kindle)
ISBN 979-8-89731-000-5 (Abridged Audio discussion)
1. Theology, Doctrinal—21st century
2. Providence and government of God

BT102 .O57 2025

This book is available in other languages at
www.DTLPress.com

Cover Image: "Jesus" in the pose of Rodin's Thinker, contemplating the universe.
Photo credit: Created by DTL Staff, using AI

Contents

Series Preface	*vii*
What is Open and Relational Theology	*1*
The Nature of God	*11*
Scripture and Revelation	*21*
Divine Love and the Problem of Evil	*33*
Human Freedom and Divine Action	*45*
Love and Salvation	*55*
Community, Church, and the Relational Body of Christ	*63*
Ethics, Justice, and Love in Action	*73*
Hope, the Future, and the Unfinished Story	*83*
Living Open and Relational Lives	*91*
Appendix: Oord's Recent Writings	*93*

Series Preface

Artificial Intelligence (AI) is changing everything, including theological scholarship and education. This series, *Theological Essentials*, is designed to bring the creative potential of AI to the field of theological education. In the traditional model, a scholar with both mastery of the scholarly discourse and a record of successful classroom teaching would spend several months—or even several years—writing, revising and rewriting an introductory text which would then be transferred to a publisher who also invested months or years in production processes. Even though the end product was typically quite predictable, this slow and expensive process caused the prices of textbooks to balloon. As a result, students in developed nations paid more than they should have for the books and students in developing nations typically had no access to these (cost-prohibitive) textbooks until they appeared as discards and donations decades later. In previous generations, the need for quality assurance—in the form of content generation, expert review, copy-editing and printing time—may have made this slow, expensive and exclusionary approach inevitable. However, AI is changing everything.

This series is very different; it is created by AI. The cover of each volume identifies the work as "created under the supervision of" an expert in the field. However, that person is not an author in the traditional sense. The creator of each volume has been trained by the DTL staff in the use of AI and *the creator has used AI to create, edit, revise and recreate the text that you see.* With that creation process clearly identified, let me explain the goals of this series.

Our Goals:

Credibility: Although AI has made—and continues to make—huge strides over the last few years, no unsupervised AI can create a truly reliable or fully credible college or seminary level text. The limitations of AI generated content sometimes originates from the limitations of the content itself (the training set may be inadequate), but more often, user dissatisfaction with AI-generated content arises from human errors associated with poor prompt engineering. The DTL Press has sought to overcome both of these problems by hiring established scholars with widely recognized expertise to create books within their areas of expertise and by training those scholars and experts in AI prompt engineering. To be clear, the scholar whose name appears on the cover of this work has created this volume—generating, reading, regenerating, rereading and revising the work. Even though the work was generated (in varying degrees) by AI, the names of our scholarly creators appear on the cover as a guarantee that the content is equally credible with any introductory work which that scholar/creator would pen using the traditional model.

Affordability: The DTL Press is committed to the idea that affordability should not be a barrier to knowledge. *All persons are equally deserving of the right to know and to understand.* Therefore, ebook versions of all DTL Press books are available from the DTL libraries without charge, and available as print books for a nominal fee. Our scholar/creators are to be thanked for their willingness to forego traditional royalty arrangements. (Our creators are compensated for their generative work, but they do not receive royalties in the traditional sense.)

Accessibility: The DTL Press would like to make high quality, low cost introductory textbooks available to everyone, everywhere in the world. The books in this series are immediately made available in multiple languages. The DTL Press will create translations in other languages upon request. Translations are, of course, generated by AI.

Our Acknowledged Limitations:

Some readers are undoubtedly thinking, "but AI can only produce derivative scholarship; AI can't create original, innovative scholarship." That criticism is, of course, largely accurate. AI is largely limited to aggregating, organizing and repackaging pre-existing ideas (although sometimes in ways that can be used to accelerate and refine the production of original scholarship). Still while acknowledging this inherent limitation of AI, the DTL Press would offer two comments: (1) Introductory texts are seldom meant to be truly ground breaking in their originality and (2) the DTL Press has other series dedicated to publishing original scholarship with traditional authorship.

Our Invitation:

The DTL Press would like to fundamentally reshape academic publishing in the theological world to make scholarship more accessible and more affordable in two ways. First, we would like to generate introductory texts in all areas of theological discourse, so that no one is ever forced to "buy a textbook" in any language. It is our vision for professors anywhere to be able to use one book, two books or an entire set of books in this series as the *introductory* textbooks for their classes. Second, we would also like to publish traditionally authored scholarly monographs for Open Access (free) distribution for an advanced scholarly readership.

Finally, the DTL Press is non-confessional and will publish works in any area of religious studies. Traditionally authored books are peer-reviewed; AI-generated introductory book creation is open to anyone with the required expertise to supervise content generation in that area of discourse. If you share the DTL Press's commitment to credibility, affordability and accessibility, contact us about changing the world of theological publishing by contributing to this series or a more traditionally authored series.

With high expectations,
Thomas E. Phillips
DTL Press Executive Director
www.thedtl.org

Chapter 1
What Is Open and Relational Theology?

Open and relational theology is a contemporary theological movement that emphasizes two central convictions: (1) God experiences time moment by moment and is therefore not immutable or impassible in the classical sense, and (2) God engages in genuinely reciprocal relationships with creation.

Open and relational theology proposes that God's nature is inherently loving, responsive, and dynamic. This view challenges certain traditional theological claims, especially those grounded in classical theism. Open and relational thinking invites us into a more participatory and hopeful understanding of divine-human interaction.

The Meaning of "Open"

The term "open" refers primarily to the future — an undetermined future not only for creatures but also for God. In this theology, the future is not predetermined or exhaustively known in every detail. Rather, it is shaped by the decisions of free creatures and the responsive love of God. This does not mean God is ignorant or uninvolved. God knows all that can be known and remains actively engaged in unfolding history.

The openness of the future makes space for authentic freedom, creativity, and risk. It also suggests that God is a co-adventurer with creation, not a distant observer pulling strings from outside of time. Open theists often contrast their view with theological determinism and meticulous providence, arguing instead that divine power is best understood as relational—persuasive, loving, and adaptable.

Open theology proposes that God's perfect knowledge includes all actualities and all possibilities. God's omniscience, therefore, is dynamic: God knows everything that can be known. As the future becomes actual, God's knowledge grows in richness and specificity. This highlights the living, moment-by-moment engagement of God with the world.

Open and relational theology reframes divine providence. Rather than planning or causing everything in advance, God works with creation in real time. God invites, inspires, warns, and partners with creatures to bring about what is good. The result is a universe filled with authentic moral responsibility, genuine relationship, and real consequences. God has aims and purposes, but these are pursued in collaboration with a world that is free and responsive. Such a framework invites believers to take their own lives seriously, knowing that their choices matter not only for themselves but for God.

The Meaning of "Relational"

To say that God is relational is to affirm that God's experience is constituted by relational love. God does not merely exist in a superficial or one-sided way; rather, God is genuinely affected by what happens in the world. Divine love is not coercive or controlling but seeks cooperation and mutuality.

This relational framework stands in contrast to classical views of divine impassibility (that God cannot be affected) and immutability (that God cannot change). Open and relational theologians affirm that while God's character is unchanging — especially God's love — God's experiences, emotions, and responses are shaped by interaction with the world.

A relational God is not aloof or static but dynamically engaged with creation. God's love entails risk, vulnerability, and responsiveness. Just as human relationships involve listening, adapting, and being moved by others, so too does God's relationship with the world involve real give-and-receive. This does not make God dependent or limited in a problematic way but underscores the richness and depth of divine love.

In the open and relational view, God's identity is not threatened by relationality; it is fulfilled by it. God's faithfulness is expressed not by unchangeability but by God's unwavering commitment to be present, compassionate, and involved. God celebrates with the joyful and grieves with the suffering, and divine emotions are not flaws to be overcome but features of divine perfection.

Divine relationality reshapes how we understand doctrines such as grace, judgment, and covenant. Grace becomes a continuous, relational gift rather than a one-time transaction. Judgment becomes a function of God's desire to restore rather than punish. Covenant becomes a mutual commitment grounded in love and trust. In all of these, God's relational nature invites humanity into a partnership that is both personal and transformative.

Historical and Theological Roots

While the open and relational approach has gained traction in recent decades, it draws on a wide and deep range of theological traditions. Many of the core convictions of open and relational theology can be traced to the biblical witness itself, where God is portrayed as dialogical, responsive, and emotionally involved. In the Hebrew Scriptures, God is seen negotiating with Abraham, grieving over human sinfulness, and changing plans in response to human intercession. The Psalms give voice to a God who listens, empathizes, and acts in the context of covenantal love.

In the New Testament, the clearest example of divine relationality is found in the incarnation. In Jesus Christ, God takes on flesh, suffers, rejoices, weeps, and ultimately dies in solidarity with creation. The Gospels consistently depict Jesus as someone who responds to others, is moved with compassion, and changes course when prompted by faith or need. The Spirit, likewise, is active within creation, groaning with it and empowering responsive, co-creative participation.

While most open and relational believers are Christian, there are also open and relational Bahai,

Jews, Muslims, and others. Rather than a problem, open and relational thinkers see the compatibility of this vision of God across religions as a gift.

Historically, open and relational theology resonates with certain strands of early Christian thought and the theology of the early church fathers, particularly in Eastern traditions that emphasized theosis and the participatory nature of salvation. It also echoes medieval mysticism and the emphasis on divine love and intimacy.

In more recent theology, figures like John Wesley have been influential, especially in their emphasis on prevenient grace and cooperative salvation. Wesleyan and Arminian traditions have long affirmed the importance of human freedom and divine responsiveness.

The rise of process theology in the 20th century—particularly through thinkers like Alfred North Whitehead and Charles Hartshorne—provided philosophical models for understanding divine relationality and temporality. While open and relational theologians differ among themselves on how much to embrace from process theology (e.g., the nature of divine power), they share a commitment to a God who is deeply affected by the world.

Philosophically, personalism and existentialism laid important groundwork. Thinkers like Martin Buber and Gabriel Marcel emphasized dialogical existence and interpersonal relationships as central to human life, which open and relational theologians have extended to the divine-human relationship. Meanwhile, developments in science—especially in quantum mechanics, chaos theory, and systems theory—have reinforced the plausibility of a world that is open, indeterminate, and relationally constituted. These insights challenge rigid mechanistic or deterministic worldviews and encourage a vision of reality that is in dynamic interaction with God.

Thus, open and relational theology emerges as both a retrieval and a reformulation. It retrieves neglected biblical and historical insights into God's loving and responsive nature, while reformulating these convictions in light of contemporary philosophical and scientific developments. It is a theology rooted in tradition and yet fully engaged with the complexities of the modern world.

Contrasts with Classical Theism

Classical theism, as shaped by figures like Augustine, Anselm, and Aquinas, is not a form of open and relational theology. Classical theism affirms divine attributes such as timelessness, immutability, impassibility, and exhaustive foreknowledge. God is conceived as the "unmoved mover"—eternally perfect, wholly transcendent, and unaffected by temporal change. God exists outside of time, perceives all of history in a single eternal present, and cannot be influenced by creation in any meaningful way. These attributes were often adopted to safeguard God's perfection, simplicity, and omnipotence.

Classical theism's portrayal of God emphasizes control, certainty, and divine self-sufficiency. God's knowledge is exhaustive and unchanging, and divine action is interpreted as either directly causing all things or predetermining with a fixed divine plan. This model of God raises significant questions—especially in relation to suffering, freedom, and divine love.

Open and relational theology offers a critical yet constructive alternative. It affirms that God's greatness is not diminished by change or relationality, but enhanced by them. Rather than viewing God as unaffected and detached, open and relational theologians propose a God who is supremely loving, deeply engaged, and temporally present. God is seen not as the unmoved mover, but as the most moved mover—a being whose essential nature is love.

This contrast is not merely metaphysical; it has pastoral and ethical implications. In a world marked by suffering, the image of a God who cannot be moved or affected may feel distant or indifferent. Open and relational theology seeks to offer a more intimate, responsive, and compassionate vision of God—one who walks with us through uncertainty and empowers us to shape the future together.

Open and relational theology reformulates theology in light of the biblical witness, the lived experience of faith, and contemporary understandings of the world. It affirms God as supremely loving, deeply engaged, and temporally present. This God is not threatened by change or vulnerability but embraces them as necessary conditions for authentic love.

Why It Matters

The theological vision presented by open and relational thinkers has profound implications for prayer, providence, suffering, and discipleship. If God truly responds, then our prayers matter — not as ritual obligations or symbolic gestures, but as real interactions that influence God and the unfolding of events. Prayer becomes a form of co-creative dialogue, a means by which God's purposes are discerned and enacted in the world.

If the future is not fixed, then our choices contribute to what unfolds. This elevates human agency and reinforces moral responsibility. Open and relational theology affirms that we are not puppets enacting a divine script, but participants in an ongoing story. Our actions matter to God and to the world, and our relationships — personal, communal, and ecological — are the arenas in which divine love is realized.

If God suffers with us, then divine love is more than abstract benevolence — it is deeply empathetic and active. In the face of tragedy, the image of a God who grieves, who feels, and who walks with us can offer a more powerful source of comfort and solidarity than a God who remains unmoved. This shifts theodicy from the question of why God allows suffering to how God shares in it and works to bring healing through cooperative means.

Instead of seeking control or certainty, open and relational theology invites us to a spirituality of trust, discernment, and responsiveness. Faith becomes less about affirming timeless propositions and more about cultivating relationship—with God, with others, and with the created world. This fosters a form of discipleship that is adaptive, courageous, and deeply engaged.

This vision nurtures a theology of hope. Rather than resigning ourselves to a predetermined fate or inscrutable divine plan, we are invited to co-create the future with God. Hope, in this light, is not passive but participatory. It trusts that God always works for good—not by overriding freedom, but by empowering love.

Open and relational theology offers a compelling and faithful way to think about a God who is love in action—a God who is with us, for us, and inviting us into the work of renewal and transformation.

Chapter 2
The Nature of God

At the heart of open and relational theology lies a transformative vision of who God is. This vision departs from classical metaphysical concepts of deity—such as absolute immutability, impassibility, and timelessness—and instead presents a God who is relational, responsive, and dynamic. Far from diminishing God's greatness, this reframing amplifies God's love, presence, and fidelity. In this chapter, we explore how open and relational theology understands the divine nature in terms of love, power, knowledge, and temporality.

Divine Love as Essential and Relational

Love is not simply one attribute among many for God—it is the essence of who God is. In open and relational theology, divine love is not abstract or impersonal; it is deeply relational and actively engaged. God is not a distant deity dispensing love from on high but a relational presence who shares in the joys and sufferings of creation.

Central to this vision is the idea that God's love is pluriform—that is, expressed in many forms depending on the context and needs of the relationship. Sometimes love looks like comfort and healing; other times it takes the form of challenge, confrontation, or justice-seeking. In every case, God's love is tailored to the flourishing of the other, reflecting the dynamic nature of real relationship.

This pluriformity does not imply inconsistency or changeability in God's character. Instead, it points to a love that is creative, wise, and situationally responsive. Just as a parent's love may express itself differently toward a grieving child than toward a rebellious teenager, so too does God's love manifest in diverse ways, depending on what is needed. Open and relational theology insists that God's love is always consistent in its intent—to promote the well-being of all—but multifaceted in its expression.

Thomas Jay Oord calls the flexible and steadfast aspects of God the divine essence-experience binate. This a conceptual framework distinguishes between God's unchanging essence and God's changing experiences. According to this model, God's essential nature is eternal, steadfast, and unalterable—especially in regard to divine love. God will always be loving, just, good, and faithful.

However, God's experiences are not fixed—they are shaped by ongoing relationships with a dynamic and unfolding world. As creation changes, suffers, rejoices, and evolves, God feels and responds accordingly. God's experience is enriched (or wounded) by what happens in time, even as God's essence remains loving and constant. In this view, God's essence guarantees stability and integrity, while God's experience allows for empathy, responsiveness, and genuine interaction. Together, the notions of pluriform love and the essence-experience binate paint a portrait of a God who is both utterly reliable and deeply engaged. God's love is not locked in a rigid form, nor is it a passive sentiment. It is active, contextual, and participatory. It listens, feels, adapts, and transforms—always aimed at healing, reconciling, and co-creating a better future.

In a world of complexity, such a vision of God offers hope. It affirms that divine love is not overwhelmed by tragedy or reduced to sentimentality. Instead, it is strong enough to suffer with us and flexible enough to meet us where we are. God's pluriform love assures us that we are neither abandoned nor coerced—we are known, valued, and invited into a living, loving relationship.

Divine Power as Persuasive and Cooperative

One of the most distinctive and provocative contributions of open and relational theology is its reimagining of divine power. Traditional Christian theology has often portrayed God's power as unilateral, overwhelming, and absolute—a divine omnipotence that can override any creature or natural law. But this picture leads to theological tensions: if God has the power to stop evil and suffering but chooses not to, what does that say about God's love?

Open and relational theology addresses this by offering a different vision: divine power as persuasive, cooperative, and noncoercive. In this view, God's power is not defined by the ability to control but by the capacity to love in ways that invite, influence, and empower. Love, by its very nature, cannot be coercive. It must allow for response, freedom, and even rejection.

Thomas Jay Oord argues that divine power is best understood not as omnipotence (all-controlling power) but as amipotence—a term coined from *ami-* (love) and *potentia* (power), meaning "the power of uncontrolling love." Amipotence says God's way of acting is always loving and never violates the integrity or freedom of others.

This understanding is grounded in the biblical witness. Throughout Scripture, God does not impose divine will through force but works through call, covenant, persuasion, and relationship. God woos Israel rather than compelling obedience. Jesus embodies divine power not through domination, but through service, sacrifice, and solidarity with the vulnerable. The cross becomes the fullest revelation of God's power—a kenotic (self-emptying) love that gives rather than grasps.

Kenosis, derived from Philippians 2:5–11, refers to Christ "emptying" himself in humility and becoming obedient unto death. *Kenosis* is self-giving, others-empowering love. Open and relational theology sees *kenosis* not as a temporary act but as a revelation of God's eternal character. God's power is always kenotic—always self-giving, cooperative, and others-empowering.

Building on this idea, theologians like Thomas Jay Oord have developed the concept of essential *kenosis*, which holds that God's self-giving love is essential to God's nature. God does not *choose* to act noncoercively; God *must* act this way. God's very essence is uncontrolling love. Essential *kenosis* maintains that God's nature of love rejects the way of control. This is not because God lacks power, but because control contradicts who God eternally is.

Amipotence means that God empowers creatures, works through processes, calls communities, and sustains life. God never bypasses the laws of nature or the freedom of persons but works within and through them to bring about healing, justice, and transformation. This vision honors both God's ongoing presence and the world's authentic freedom.

In this framework, divine power is not about intervention from outside creation but about constant, cooperative engagement from within. God is the most influential and maximally powerful, but divine influence respects the agency and complexity of the world. And though God's aims are sometimes thwarted—because others can say no—God never gives up.

Amipotence and essential *kenosis* invite a radical trust in God's character, even when outcomes are painful or uncertain. They allow us to say that God is always doing all that divine love can do in every moment, without violating the freedom and integrity of creation. Divine power, then, is collaborative rather than coercive, relational rather than unilateral, and eternally faithful even when the world resists.

Divine Knowledge as Dynamic and Open

In open and relational theology, God's knowledge is understood not as static and all-determined, but as dynamic, relational, and open to the unfolding future. This view maintains that God knows all that can be known—but because the future includes genuine possibilities rather than fixed certainties, even God does not know with certainty what will happen. This is not a deficiency in God but a consequence of the nature of reality.

At the heart of this vision is a commitment to an open future—the belief that the future is not settled but contains real possibilities. Rather than imagining history as a completed script or divine blueprint waiting to be played out, open and relational theology proposes that the future is partly indeterminate. God, along with creatures, participates in its ongoing formation. This view of time resists both fatalism and determinism, affirming instead a world in which genuine freedom, novelty, and change are real.

God's omniscience, therefore, includes complete knowledge of the past and present, as well as an exhaustive grasp of every possible future outcome. God knows all conceivable paths forward, every contingency, and every potentiality. God's knowledge is not reduced to a cosmic forecast; it is a relational awareness that embraces both what is and what could be, in every moment.

This model of divine knowledge underscores God's attentiveness and wisdom. God does not passively watch the future unfold but is actively engaged, adapting in real time to creaturely decisions, environmental shifts, and unfolding events. Faith is not about clinging to deterministic outcomes or rigid expectations but about trusting a God who is wise, present, and capable in the midst of change.

The open and relational theology view resonates with Scripture. The biblical God often expresses surprise, changes course, grieves over outcomes, or celebrates unexpected faith. God responds to Nineveh's repentance, regrets making Saul king, and marvels at the centurion's faith. Such stories suggest not a fixed future or an all-determined plan, but a living God in a living world.

In summary, open and relational theology presents divine knowledge as perfectly suited to a relational universe. God knows all that is and all that could be. Rather than being the omniscient controller of a closed system, God is the infinitely wise companion of a world still becoming.

Divine Temporality and Immanence

A central affirmation of open and relational theology is that God experiences time. Unlike classical theism, which portrays God as timeless — existing outside of past, present, and future — open and relational thought insists that God is temporal in the most meaningful sense: God lives moment by moment, just as creatures do.

To say that God is temporal is to affirm that God participates in the ongoing unfolding of reality. God remembers the past, is fully present in the now, and anticipates the future. Divine memory is perfect and unfading; divine anticipation is richly imaginative and wise.

This temporality is essential to divine relationality. If God did not experience change, sequence, or anticipation, it would be difficult to imagine how genuine relationship with creation could occur. Love requires some form of temporal awareness. The God who rejoices, grieves, listens, and responds must be a God who is *with us in time*, not apart from it.

God's presence in time also gives theological depth to the concept of divine immanence. God is not only transcendent—beyond all things—but also intimately near, involved in the smallest and most personal moments of existence. This leads to a vision of relational transcendence: God transcends the world not by being detached from it, but by being more deeply connected to it than anything else could be. God's transcendence is not a spatial separation but a qualitative distinction.

Such a view finds support throughout Scripture. The biblical narrative consistently portrays God as a participant in time-bound events: making covenants, reacting to prayers, responding to sin, and bringing about new beginnings. Jesus himself embodies temporality: he grows, weeps, rejoices, waits, suffers, and dies. In Christ, God's presence in time is not only affirmed—it is celebrated.

What happens in time is not a shadow of eternal truths but the very sphere in which God acts and relates. Events matter. Relationships matter. Decisions matter. Time is not a prison to escape or a problem to solve—it is the very medium of divine love.

In open and relational theology, time is not a threat to God's perfection but a gift that allows for the richness of relationship. God is the God of becoming—not because God is incomplete, but because God is eternally committed to a world that is still becoming what it is meant to be. God's faithfulness is not the refusal to change, but the refusal to give up.

Conclusion

Open and relational theology invites us to reimagine the nature of God in ways that are faithful to Scripture, responsive to lived experience, and attentive to the complexity of the world. In contrast to classical views that emphasize divine distance, immutability, and control, this theology presents a God who is profoundly loving, persuasive, knowledgeable, and present.

God's love is not static or impersonal, but pluriform—expressed in diverse and contextually wise ways. God's power is not coercive but kenotic and amipotent: a self-giving strength that seeks cooperation and transformation rather than domination. God's knowledge is not exhaustive in the classical sense of a fixed future, but dynamic and open—deeply attuned to what is, and infinitely imaginative about what could be. And God is not timelessly detached but temporally present, faithfully participating in the unfolding of history and the rhythms of relationship.

This vision of God affirms divine greatness not in isolation or control, but in relational love. It's a theology capable of addressing the deepest questions not by retreating into mystery, but by pointing to a God who is always with us, always working for good, and always inviting us into the co-creation of a more loving world.

Chapter 3
Scripture and Revelation

If God is relational, responsive, and open to the future, then our understanding of divine revelation—and particularly of Scripture—must reflect that vision. In open and relational theology, Scripture is not seen as a static deposit of timeless truths or a divinely dictated manual. Instead, it is a dynamic testimony to the ongoing relationship between God and creation. The Bible bears witness to a God who speaks, listens, reacts, and participates—a God who reveals love.

This chapter explores how open and relational theology approaches the nature of Scripture, how it interprets the Bible's portrayal of God, and how it handles difficult or morally troubling texts. At the heart of this approach is the belief that revelation is not merely propositional or informational—it is relational, narrative, and dialogical.

Scripture as Relational Witness

In open and relational theology, Scripture is best understood as a relational witness—a record of divine-human interaction that reflects the evolving, dynamic nature of God's relationship with creation. The Bible does not give us a sterile list of facts or an abstract philosophical system. Rather, it tells the story of a God who engages creation in time, responds to human freedom, and is deeply affected by the joys and sorrows of the world.

This approach sees Scripture as both divinely inspired and humanly composed. God worked with people, in their particular historical and cultural settings, to reveal divine character through the stories, songs, laws, prayers, visions, and teachings that comprise the biblical canon. As such, the Bible is not a divine monologue but a dialogue.

A classic example of this relational dynamic can be found in Genesis 18, where Abraham intercedes for the city of Sodom. Abraham engages God in a bold negotiation, and God listens, responds, and adjusts the divine plan based on Abraham's appeal. This exchange illustrates not only Abraham's courage but also God's willingness to be influenced by human reasoning.

Another key instance is found in Exodus 32, where Moses pleads with God to spare the Israelites after their idolatry with the golden calf. The text states: *"Then the Lord relented and did not bring on his people the disaster he had threatened"* (Exodus 32:14, NIV). Moses' intercession matters. God is portrayed not as rigid and immovable, but as willing to adjust divine intentions in light of covenantal relationship.

In the prophetic literature, God is often depicted as deeply invested in the fate of Israel and the nations. The book of Hosea portrays God's anguish and compassion with searing imagery: *"My heart is changed within me; all my compassion is aroused"* (Hosea 11:8). This is a God of deep relational pathos.

The Psalms, too, model an open and relational engagement with God. The psalmists often cry out in complaint, plea, or praise, assuming that God hears and responds in real time. Psalm 13, for example, begins with a lament — *"How long, O Lord? Will you forget me forever?"* — but ends with a statement of trust in God's unfailing love. These prayers arise from a conviction that God is not unmoved or aloof, but attentive and engaged.

The dynamic quality of Scripture is evident in the way God's character is progressively revealed over time. The earlier parts of the Old Testament often depict God using language of judgment, warfare, and retribution — reflecting ancient cultural understandings of power. Yet as the narrative unfolds, we see increasing emphasis on mercy, compassion, and nonviolence. The prophet Micah summarizes this trajectory: *"What does the Lord require of you? To act justly and to love mercy and to walk humbly with your God"* (Micah 6:8).

In the New Testament, Jesus reveals the fullness of God's relational nature. In Jesus, we see divine power exercised through humility, service, healing, and inclusion. Jesus embodies a God who touches lepers (Mark 1:40-42), weeps over the death of a friend (John 11:35), and forgives enemies from the cross (Luke 23:34). The incarnation itself is the ultimate act of relational love.

Rather than flattening Scripture into a uniform codebook, open and relational theology treats the Bible as a living testimony — a layered, evolving conversation between God and God's people. Different voices and genres reflect the complexity of that relationship.

In short, Scripture functions not as a fixed blueprint but as a relational guide, helping readers and communities enter into their own journey with God. It testifies to a God who calls, listens, adapts, and persists—and who continues to reveal love through relationship today.

The Bible's Portrayal of a Relational God

One of the central affirmations of open and relational theology is that the Bible consistently portrays God not a static, impassible force, but a living presence who engages with creation in meaningful, mutual relationship. God is a participant in the unfolding story of the world.

Throughout Scripture, we see a God who speaks and listens, who enters into covenants, and who is emotionally invested in creation. Far from presenting a deity immune to suffering or change, the Bible reveals a God who is affected by the actions of others, and who adjusts plans and responses accordingly.

Consider Genesis 6:6, where God observes the violence and corruption of humanity and *"regretted that he had made human beings on the earth, and his heart was deeply troubled."* This moment is striking: the Creator is not removed from creation's trajectory but is grieved by it. The text suggests that God is heartbroken by how events unfold.

In Jeremiah 18, the prophet is sent to the potter's house, where God offers a metaphor for divine flexibility. *"If at any time I announce that a nation or kingdom is to be uprooted… but if that nation repents… then I will relent"* (Jeremiah 18:7-8). Here, God explicitly states that divine action is conditional upon human response. The future is not locked in; it is shaped by the interplay between divine intention and creaturely decision.

This same dynamic is evident in the story of Jonah, where God sends a reluctant prophet to proclaim judgment to Nineveh. But when the people repent, *"God relented from the disaster he had threatened"* (Jonah 3:10). Jonah's frustration stems from the fact that he knows God is gracious and responsive, not rigid and deterministic: *"I knew that you are a gracious and compassionate God, slow to anger and abounding in love…"* (Jonah 4:2). The entire narrative affirms God's relational responsiveness to human actions.

The New Testament continues and intensifies this theme, most clearly in the life of Jesus. The Gospels present him as the fullest revelation of God's nature. In Jesus, we see a relational God made visible: one who touches the unclean (Mark 1:41), honors the faith of outsiders (Matthew 8:10), and is moved by human suffering (Luke 7:13).

One particularly compelling episode occurs in Mark 7:24-30, where a Syrophoenician woman pleads with Jesus to heal her daughter. Initially, Jesus seems to resist, referencing the "children's bread" and the "dogs." But the woman responds with wit and faith, and Jesus changes course, affirming her faith and healing her daughter. Jesus is not performing a scripted miracle but participating in an encounter of mutual engagement.

Jesus also models divine grief and vulnerability. In John 11:35, we are told simply, *"Jesus wept."* The tears are not performative but expressive of deep compassion. God is not a stoic deity who transcends emotion; in Jesus, God shares in the full range of human experience, revealing a divine heart that feels deeply and acts in solidarity.

The apostle Paul describes the Spirit of God as an active, emotional presence within the world. In Romans 8:26–27, the Spirit is said to intercede with *"groans too deep for words."* The Spirit participates in the world's pain, joining creation in longing and hope.

Taken together, these texts portray a God who is far from the "unmoved mover" of classical theism. Instead, the God of Scripture is the most moved mover—not passive or reactive, but deeply and willingly responsive. God's relationality is a strength rooted in divine love.

God's responsiveness does not suggest inconsistency or capriciousness. Rather, it reflects a stable character of love expressed in flexible ways. God's moral commitments—to justice, mercy, fidelity, and redemption—remain steadfast. But how those commitments are enacted varies in response to the complexities of human history and interaction. This is pluriform love in action.

Reading Scripture with an Open and Relational Hermeneutic

To read the Bible through an open and relational lens is to approach Scripture as a living conversation between God and humanity—a relational document that continues to speak, challenge, and invite us into participation. Scripture is best understood through the unfolding drama of God's loving engagement with creation across time.

A relational hermeneutic begins with the conviction that God's self-revelation is dynamic and contextual. The Bible is not a dropped-from-the-sky divine transcript; it is a Spirit-inspired compilation shaped by the particularities of human communities in relationship with God. Just as God meets people where they are, the biblical texts reflect the developmental, dialogical process of revelation—often messy, contested, and evolving.

In certain cases—especially those involving violence, patriarchy, or harsh retributive justice—open and relational theology urges readers to discern the divine trajectory within the text rather than assuming every verse equally reveals God's character. Scripture shows humanity in the process of learning what God is like—not always getting it right, but growing toward greater clarity over time.

Many Christians in open and relational theology adopt a Christ-centered interpretive approach. Jesus is the clearest and fullest revelation of God (Hebrews 1:1–3; John 1:14–18), and as such, he becomes the hermeneutical key for understanding Scripture. Most open and relational theologians affirm that the life, teachings, death, and resurrection of Jesus reveal God's relational, noncoercive, self-giving love. Any passage that appears to contradict the character of God revealed in Christ must be read critically, contextually, and with moral and theological discernment.

One particularly influential version of this approach is Gregory Boyd's cruciform hermeneutic, developed most fully in his work *The Crucifixion of the Warrior God*. Boyd argues that Scripture should be interpreted through the lens of the cross—that is, God's supreme revelation of self-giving, nonviolent love in Jesus' death. Even passages that portray God as violent or retributive can be understood by what they point to when seen through the cruciform lens. Just as God "stooped" to meet humanity in the incarnation, God also stoops to bear the misunderstandings and limitations of ancient peoples in Scripture.

For Boyd, the Bible is not a sanitized record of God's actions but a testimony to God's humble willingness to be misrepresented within a fallen. Thus, the cross not only saves—it becomes the lens through which all Scripture must be read, especially the troubling parts. Boyd's approach reinforces the idea that Scripture, like all divine communication, happens in relationship—accommodating, adapting, and patiently drawing humanity forward, even through broken understandings.

This hermeneutic also embraces the narrative arc of Scripture. Rather than flattening the Bible into a uniform moral or theological code, it recognizes that Scripture unfolds over time, often through tension and transformation. Early portrayals of God as a tribal warrior or harsh judge must be held in dialogue with later visions of God as forgiving, inclusive, and sacrificially loving. The Bible itself contains multiple voices, and it often records the struggle of God's people to understand, follow, and represent God faithfully.

Take, for example, the contrast between the conquest narratives of Joshua and the prophetic calls for justice and peace in Isaiah and Micah. Or the contrast between David's military exploits and Jesus' call to nonviolence. A relational reading asks: how does this part of the story contribute to the whole? Is it descriptive or prescriptive? How does it align with the God we see in Jesus?

This approach also invites moral discernment—a central feature of any theology that takes human freedom and divine partnership seriously. Ethical questions—such as how to think about slavery, women in leadership, sexuality, or ecological responsibility—cannot be answered by quoting verses alone. They require thoughtful engagement with the broader narrative of divine love, justice, and liberation.

In this sense, Scripture becomes a participatory space. Reading Scripture relationally means being willing to wrestle, question, and grow. It means trusting that God is not threatened by our questions, nor confined by ancient categories, but continues to speak in fresh, faithful ways. The same God who inspired the words of ancient prophets and apostles is still working, still speaking, and still inviting us into the story.

Ongoing Revelation and Participatory Faith

The authority of Scripture is best understood not in terms of fixed propositions but in terms of its ability to bear faithful witness to a living, relational God. The Bible tells the story of God's engagement with people in particular times and places—and it invites each generation to take up that story, not by repeating it verbatim, but by discerning how God is moving in the present.

The work of Walter Brueggemann is especially helpful here. Brueggemann emphasizes that the Bible is not a single, settled narrative but a polyphonic, dialogical text—filled with tension, contradiction, and competing voices. He resists attempts to systematize Scripture or to reduce it to a singular theological message. Instead, he describes the Bible as a "conversation" and a "testimony," with diverse human responses to God over time.

Brueggemann's notion of the "prophetic imagination" helps readers see that Scripture is not merely descriptive of what is, but invitational—calling communities into new ways of thinking, acting, and relating. He encourages reading the Bible with attentiveness to context, voice, and genre, and urges modern readers to join the ongoing process of interpretation as faithful participants. His work resonates strongly with open and relational theology in its refusal to freeze the text or to idolize certainty.

Similarly, Eric Seibert challenges the assumption that every portrait of God in Scripture equally reflects divine character. In books like *Disturbing Divine Behavior*, Seibert draws a distinction between "the textual God" and "the actual God"—recognizing that many depictions of divine violence or harshness likely reflect human perceptions rather than divine reality. Rather than denying or explaining away troubling texts, Seibert proposes that we engage them critically, theologically, and ethically.

This openness to ongoing revelation fosters participatory faith. Faith is active partnership in God's ongoing work of love and justice. The Spirit who inspired the prophets and apostles continues to speak today—through the gathered community, through acts of compassion, through art, science, nature, protest, and prayer.

This vision also reinforces the idea that theology itself is contextual and unfolding. We are not called to replicate the past, but to carry forward its spirit into the present. The church, then, becomes not a museum of divine words but a living body—a community of ongoing interpretation.

Conclusion

Open and relational theology views Scripture not as a closed script but as a relational narrative. The Spirit uses the Bible to invite us into relationship. God's revelation is ongoing, interpretation is dynamic, and discipleship is deeply participatory.

This approach challenges simplistic readings of the Bible while remaining deeply faithful to its core message: that God is love, and that this love is always reaching, always responding, and always inviting us into the unfolding story of grace.

Chapter 4
Divine Love and the Problem of Evil

Few questions cut deeper into the heart of theology than the problem of evil. If God is all-powerful and all-loving, why does suffering persist? Why do tragedies occur? Why doesn't God stop them? For many, these questions are not abstract puzzles but lived experiences. They lie at the center of grief, trauma, and spiritual crisis.

Classical theology often addresses this tension with appeals to mystery, sovereignty, or divine plans hidden from human understanding. But open and relational theology refuses to accept an image of God that is either indifferent or complicit in suffering. Instead, many open and relational theologians begin with a bold conviction: God's power is best understood not as coercive force, but as relentless, persuasive, co-suffering love.

This chapter explores how open and relational theology reimagines divine power and proposes a vision of providence that takes both love and evil seriously.

The Classical Question

Traditionally, the problem of evil is framed as a trilemma: If God is all-powerful, God could prevent evil. If God is all-loving, God would want to prevent evil. But evil happens.

This formulation exposes the tension at the heart of much classical theology. If God can do anything, why doesn't God stop genocides, childhood cancer, natural disasters, or abuse? Appeals to divine mystery or greater good come at the cost of credibility and ethical coherence.

Open and relational asks a different set of questions: What kind of power is consistent with love? What kind of love refuses to override the freedom of others? What if God's love is the reason God cannot prevent all evil?

The God Who Cannot Coerce

At the heart of open and relational theology is a transformative rethinking of divine power. Instead of imagining God as a sovereign ruler who could unilaterally prevent evil but chooses not to, this theology insists that God's very nature is love—and love, by definition, does not coerce.

This idea is expressed most clearly in the concept of essential *kenosis*, a theological model developed by Thomas Jay Oord. *Kenosis*, drawn from Philippians 2:5–8, describes the self-giving love of Christ—a love that humbles itself, takes the form of a servant, and suffers with and for others. Essential *kenosis* goes further, proposing that this self-giving, others-empowering love is not just how God chooses to act—it is who God eternally is. God's very essence is kenotic love.

If love is God's essential nature, then God must always act in ways that are consistent with that love. And if genuine love refuses to override the will, agency, or integrity of others, then divine action must always be noncoercive. God cannot contradict God's own nature by forcefully overriding creaturely freedom or the structures of creation. God invites, calls, persuades, and inspires—but never controls.

This idea leads to a radically hopeful reframing of divine power as amipotence—a term combining *amare* (to love) and *potentia* (power). Amipotence is God's power of uncontrolling love. Amipotence redefines power as the unwavering ability to love, influence, and empower in all circumstances. God cannot override or overpower but cooperates and empowers others.

This means that when evil occurs—whether through moral wrongdoing, natural disasters, or systemic injustice—it is not because God is passive, indifferent, or testing us. Nor is it because God "permits" evil for some hidden purpose. Rather, God always acts to prevent harm and promote healing, but the conditions of creaturely freedom and complex systems sometimes resist or obstruct God's desires.

This reframing preserves God's goodness while honestly acknowledging the brokenness of the world. It also avoids the deeply problematic idea that God "allows" evil for a greater good. In contrast, God is never the cause of or inactive bystander to evil, but its fiercest opponent— present in every moment, working to redeem, to restore, and to empower healing.

Open and relational thinkers typically say God is the most influential being in the universe—ever-present, ever-loving, ever-creative. But God's influence is exerted not through brute force but through relational fidelity, offering the best possible options in each moment, adapting to creation's choices, and patiently guiding history toward healing.

This vision aligns with Scripture. In the Gospels, Jesus never coerces. He invites disciples to follow, teaches with parables, responds to faith, and walks away from those who reject him. Even his miracles occur in the context of relationship, faith, and consent. The cross is the ultimate expression of divine power—not in domination, but in vulnerable, sacrificial love.

Pastorally, the implications are profound. In moments of suffering, open and relational theology proclaims that God is not the cause of your pain, nor a passive spectator. God is with you. God is grieving with you. God is doing all that divine love can do in that moment to bring healing, justice, and renewal—without violating the freedom that makes love possible in the first place.

In short, the God who cannot coerce is not weak. This God never abandons, never manipulates, and never stops working for the good. Such a vision offers a consistent, compassionate, and relational view of God of uncontrolling love.

Freedom, Risk, and the Logic of Love

If God desires authentic, mutual relationship with creation, God must grant genuine freedom to creatures—freedom to respond, resist, grow, fail, flourish, or rebel. The possibility of love necessarily includes the possibility of harm. As a result, a world built for relationship is also a world of risk.

Open and relational thinkers argue that freedom is not a temporary condition or an illusion; it is a permanent feature of how God relates to the world. Love that coerces is no love at all. Therefore, God cannot guarantee outcomes or force obedience without violating the very freedom that makes love and moral responsibility meaningful.

This perspective aligns with the biblical witness. In Genesis, Adam and Eve are given freedom in the garden—not just to obey, but to choose, even to disobey (Genesis 2-3). God warns, advises, and instructs, but does not prevent their choice. In Deuteronomy, Moses says to the people, *"I have set before you life and death, blessing and curse. Choose life"* (Deuteronomy 30:19). The invitation to relationship always comes with the freedom to do otherwise.

Freedom means that creation is not scripted. The future is not predetermined. Instead, it unfolds moment by moment in a relational web of decisions, interactions, and responses. Each creature plays a role in shaping the future alongside God and others. In short, love requires freedom, and freedom involves risk.

But this risk is not recklessness. It is the risk taken by any parent, lover, or friend in real relationship. God, in this view, is the ultimate relational partner—offering presence, guidance, wisdom, and power that persuades but never compels. This is not the absence of power, but a different kind of power altogether: one that trusts the potential of others, even at great cost.

Open and relational theology emphasizes that God does not create a world and then step back to let it run. Divine action is constant and ever-present. God is always offering the best possibilities, the wisest paths, the most loving options. But whether those are realized depends not just on God, but on how creation responds. When tragedies occur, it is not because God failed to act, but because the world is truly participatory, and freedom means that things can go horribly wrong.

This also includes the freedom and indeterminacy of nonhuman creation. Natural processes—like tectonic activity, evolution, or genetic mutation—are necessary features of a dynamic, life-producing world. But these same processes can result in earthquakes, pandemics, or disease. God does not micro-manage molecules any more than God micromanages human choices.

Open and relational theology recognizes that a world full of relational possibility is also a world full of uncertainty. But in this uncertainty, God remains the most faithful presence—not pulling strings behind the scenes, but working in real time with real agents toward healing and hope. This framework supports an ethically serious spirituality. If God does not control outcomes, then what we do really matters. Human agency is not symbolic—it's vital. We are called to partner with

God in resisting evil, seeking justice, and cultivating the good.

The God Who Suffers With Us

One of the most powerful affirmations in open and relational theology is that God suffers with creation. Unlike classical theism, which has often emphasized God's impassibility (the idea that God does not experience emotional change or suffering), open and relational theology insists that God is deeply moved by the world, affected by its joy and pain, and intimately present in its suffering.

This vision of God finds deep resonance in Scripture. The God of the Bible is not detached or untouched. God hears the cries of the oppressed in Egypt (Exodus 3:7), grieves over human violence (Genesis 6:6), mourns through the prophets (Jeremiah 8:21), and expresses longing for restoration (Hosea 11:8-9). The God of the Hebrew Bible is a covenantal God who feels, who responds, who suffers because of love.

This relational pathos reaches its fullest expression in Jesus. Jesus weeps (John 11:35), groans in anguish (Mark 14:33-36), and dies in public shame and abandonment (Mark 15:34). The incarnation of the Spirit in Jesus reveals a God of vulnerability, suffering, and solidarity with the wounded. As Jürgen Moltmann says in *The Crucified God*, "God weeps with us so that we may one day laugh with him." The cross is not a transactional mechanism of atonement, but a revelation of God's co-suffering love—a love that refuses to abandon us, even in death.

Open and relational theology builds on this insight by emphasizing that divine suffering is a reflection of God's eternal character. God always suffers with those who suffer. God is the most emotionally available being in existence—the one who feels with us, for us, and through us.

This has profound implications for both theology and pastoral care. In moments of profound loss, we may not find comfort in explanations. But we may find comfort in knowing that God is not the cause of our suffering—and that God is suffering alongside us. God is present in the ICU, in the war zone, in the collapse of relationships and systems.

This vision of God is not only emotionally powerful—it is also ethically mobilizing. If God suffers with the wounded, then to follow God is to be drawn into that same solidarity. The call of discipleship becomes a call to compassion, presence, advocacy, and healing.

This suffering love also entails divine trust. Theologian Curtis Holtzen, in his book *The God Who Trusts,* argues that God not only suffers with creation but also entrusts creation with genuine agency. God has faith in creatures—not in a naïve or detached way, but in a profoundly relational sense. This vision deepens the picture of a suffering God by showing that divine vulnerability is not limited to emotional pain but includes a willingness to trust us with the unfolding of history.

To say that God suffers with us, then, is also to say that God believes in us. God trusts that love can take root, that healing can happen, that justice can be pursued—even in the face of resistance and pain.

Providence as Relational and Redemptive

Classical models of providence often envision God as a meticulous planner or micromanager. In these frameworks, tragedy and suffering are understood as instruments in God's sovereign plan. Open and relational theology rejects this view as incompatible with a God of uncontrolling love. It offers a vision of providence that is dynamic, relational, and deeply redemptive.

God is not the unilateral architect of every event but the faithful companion who responds moment by moment, guiding creation through the complex web of relationships, choices, and natural processes. Providence is not about preordained outcomes but about God's active, loving involvement in the unfolding story of creation.

Divine action is always persuasive, invitational, and empowering—never manipulative. This means that God works with what is available, responding creatively to both beauty and brokenness. When harm or tragedy occurs—whether due to human wrongdoing, systemic injustice, or natural causes—God does not stand by passively, nor does God orchestrate pain for hidden purposes. Rather, God immediately seeks the next best possibilities for healing, justice, and redemption, given the real conditions of the world.

This view of providence highlights God's relational wisdom. God is infinitely resourceful, constantly weaving new possibilities from the tangled threads of creation's freedom and limitation. In the words of Thomas Jay Oord, "God's providence is the ongoing divine activity that empowers and invites creatures into cooperative relationships aimed at well-being."

Biblically, this understanding of providence resonates with countless stories in which God adapts and responds to unfolding circumstances. In Genesis, after human violence spreads, God grieves and begins again through Noah. In the story of Joseph, God does not prevent the betrayal by his brothers, but works within the situation to bring about good (Genesis 50:20). In the Exodus, God delivers Israel not through meticulous control but through partnership with Moses, the people, and even pagan rulers. These narratives do not portray a God who micromanages every detail but a God who works creatively with the willing and the available.

Rather than saying "everything happens for a reason," open and relational thinkers propose that everything matters to God. God is always doing all that divine love can do in every situation. This vision also calls forth creaturely agency. If God does not singlehandedly control the world, then our participation matters deeply.

This means that prayer, creativity, protest, art, technology, caregiving, peacemaking—all become acts of collaboration with divine love. As co-creators with God, we become instruments of redemption in a world that is not finished but still being made.

Conclusion

Open and relational theology offers a God who is deeply loving, deeply involved, and deeply affected by the world. This God cannot control but who never gives up. The open and relational God suffers with us, empowers us, and invites us to become agents of healing and justice.

This vision affirms the gravity of evil, the necessity of freedom, and the power of divine love. It encourages us not only to ask where God is in our suffering, but also to see ourselves as partners with God in responding to it. In the face of pain, the God of open and relational theology offers unbreakable presence, uncontrolling love, and co-creative hope.

Chapter 5
Human Freedom and Divine Action

One of the central affirmations of open and relational theology is that human freedom is real and meaningful. In contrast to theological frameworks that depict God as the ultimate cause of everything — including human choices — open and relational theology paints a picture of a God who lovingly empowers creation and invites cooperation. This chapter explores how human freedom and divine action function together in a world marked by relationship, risk, and creative potential.

Human Freedom: The Gift and the Risk

Open and relational theology affirms that freedom is not merely a philosophical concept — it is woven into the fabric of creation. God's intention for the world has been shaped by love, and love requires freedom. Control may produce compliance, but it can never create communion. Love that is forced ceases to be love at all.

Freedom is a central feature of what it means to be created in the image of God. To be human is to be capable of making choices that shape our lives, our communities, and even the world itself. But the gift of freedom is not restricted to human beings. Most open and relational theologians often extend this agency to other forms of creation as well—to animals, ecosystems, and the dynamic structures of the universe. The world is not a passive stage on which God performs, but a network of living relationships, each with a degree of responsiveness and influence.

This emphasis on genuine freedom stands in contrast to theological systems that prioritize divine control, predestination, or meticulous sovereignty. In such systems, human choices may appear free on the surface but are ultimately folded into a divine plan that cannot be altered. Open and relational theology challenges this view by insisting that freedom is real, and the future is not settled. Our choices make a difference—not just to us, but to God and the unfolding of history.

Scripture offers rich support for this perspective. In Genesis 2-3, Adam and Eve are given moral agency in the garden. God warns them, offers guidance, and provides boundaries—but does not override their decision. The consequences are real, but so is the dignity of their freedom. In Deuteronomy 30:19, Moses presents the people with a stark choice: "I have set before you life and death, blessings and curses. Now choose life." The prophetic tradition, too, is filled with appeals to human freedom: to repent, to act justly, to return to covenantal faithfulness.

In the New Testament, Jesus consistently treats people as morally responsible agents. He calls disciples to follow but does not force them. He invites the rich young ruler to a life of radical generosity, and when the man declines, Jesus lets him walk away (Mark 10:17-22). The parables are filled with characters who must choose how to respond to invitation, crisis, or opportunity. Even the final vision of the kingdom in Revelation speaks of a renewed world in which people from all nations are drawn freely into the healing presence of God (Revelation 21-22).

Philosophically, open and relational theology affirms a libertarian view of freedom. This means that not all of our decisions are determined by biology, environment, or divine foreordination. These decisions are not scripted; they emerge from the interplay of intention, character, community, and divine influence.

Freedom allows for love, creativity, growth, and discovery — but it also opens the door to harm, failure, injustice, and tragedy. The Holocaust, slavery, ecological destruction, and personal betrayal are not "part of God's plan" — they are misuses of freedom. They grieve God. But rather than try to control creatures, God responds with the same love that made freedom possible in the first place.

Divine action is not absent in creaturely freedom but embedded in it. God offers possibilities for good, speaks through conscience and community, and gently lures creation toward flourishing. But God does not force or control.

This theology elevates the importance of human responsibility. If our choices are real, then they matter. Our moral decisions ripple outward, impacting families, systems, the environment, and future generations. They also influence God.

This view of freedom invites a spirituality of discernment and accountability, where we recognize that our lives are not accidents of fate or pieces in a puzzle. We are, instead, participants in a sacred drama—a story in which our agency matters.

Divine Action: Persistent, Persuasive Love

In open and relational theology, divine action is understood as constant, relational, and persuasive rather than occasional, detached, or coercive. God's power is not expressed through domination but through love—a love that never ceases to invite, empower, and co-create.

This vision challenges classical notions of omnipotence, which often define God's power as the ability to do absolutely anything, including override human will or natural law. Most open and relational theologians affirm instead that God's power is shaped by God's nature—and God's nature is uncontrolling love. Therefore, God acts in ways that are always consistent with love: nurturing freedom, seeking the good, and honoring the agency of all creatures.

God works through persuasion and partnership. Divine action is akin to that of a wise guide, an empowering teacher, or a nurturing friend—offering possibilities for good, nudging toward healing and justice, and adapting in real time to the decisions of others.

The biblical narrative is filled with examples of this persuasive mode of divine action. God calls Abraham and makes a covenant with him rather than forcing obedience (Genesis 12, 15). God works through Moses to confront Pharaoh rather than circumventing the political realities of Egypt (Exodus 3-14). The prophets plead with Israel to return to God, revealing a divine desire for mutual response rather than mechanical compliance. Jesus invites, teaches, and heals, but never coerces belief or allegiance. Even the Spirit is described as a gentle presence who leads, empowers, and intercedes rather than compels (Romans 8:14, 26).

This understanding means that God is always acting in every moment. Divine action is not confined to occasional miracles or supernatural interventions. Rather, it occurs in the quiet depths of relationship, the unfolding of creativity, the processes of nature, and the unfolding story of communities and cultures. God is at work in the movements of justice, the struggles for liberation, the work of healing, the beauty of art, and the rhythms of ecosystems.

God acts differently in different circumstances, because pluriform love adapts to what is possible and available. If conditions are open and receptive, God's influence may lead to dramatic transformation. If resistance or limitations prevail, God does not abandon creation, but offers the next best possibility, always seeking to redeem and renew within the bounds of freedom.

This perspective reframes the concept of providence. Instead of seeing God as the one who controls or predetermines all events, open and relational theology presents God as the one who accompanies and responds. God acts to inspire and empower not manipulate and control.

Science in an Open Universe

One of the great strengths of open and relational theology is its ability to integrate scientific understandings of the universe with a theological vision of divine love and freedom. Whereas some theologies struggle to reconcile divine sovereignty with evolutionary biology, quantum physics, or chaos theory, open and relational theology embraces these insights as confirmations of a world that is indeterminate, emergent, and richly relational.

In evolutionary science, for instance, we see that life unfolds through variation, adaptation, and openness to the environment. In quantum physics, we discover that particles behave probabilistically, not deterministically. In systems theory, we see that even small influences can ripple through complex networks in unpredictable ways. All of these scientific discoveries point toward a world that is not fixed, closed, or mechanistic, but one that is open to novelty, creativity, and meaningful change.

This scientific vision resonates with the open and relational understanding of God. God does not manipulate matter from outside or override the autonomy of natural processes. Instead, God works within and through these processes, inviting creation into greater levels of complexity, cooperation, and flourishing. Divine action is not about interrupting nature but about partnering with it in every moment.

A relational view of creation also transforms our approach to the environment. In many strands of Christian theology, nature has been treated as secondary to human salvation—a stage for moral development or a resource for human use. But open and relational theology affirms that creation is valuable in itself, not merely as a means to an end.

Environmental degradation is not merely a scientific or political issue—it is a relational and theological crisis. To damage the Earth is to harm God's beloved partners. Ecological care is not optional—it is a sacred calling. The same love that calls us into relationship with our neighbors calls us into solidarity with ecosystems, animals, and future generations.

An exciting implications of open and relational theology is the idea that creation is not finished, but still unfolding. God draws creation forward into greater beauty, diversity, and interdependence. Humans play a key role in this process. Made in the image of God, we are not passive observers but co-creators. This does not mean we take over God's work, but that we take up our place within it.

This also opens the door for a renewed theology of vocation. Our daily lives—our work, our relationships, our engagement with culture and nature—are all contexts for divine-human cooperation. We do not simply wait for God to act; we ask what God is inviting us to do, and we act accordingly. We become agents of love in an open world, shaping the future with God.

A Collaborative World

At the heart of open and relational theology is a compelling reimagination of how the world works. It is not as a closed system governed by a divine blueprint, nor as a stage upon which God performs predetermined acts. We live in an animated and collaborative world in which God and creation work together in shaping the future.

In this collaborative world, God provides the conditions for life, the guidance for goodness, and the energy for transformation. But God never singlehandedly determines outcomes. Divine action is always invitational. God offers the best possibilities in every moment, but those possibilities can only be realized when other agents—human or otherwise—respond.

This understanding draws from a rich biblical tradition. In Genesis 1, God creates a world out of chaos. Creation is then instructed to "be fruitful," to "bring forth," to multiply and fill. God does not micromanage but empowers creation to participate in its own becoming. In Exodus, God liberates Israel not through sheer force, but in partnership with Moses and a newly formed community. In the Gospels, Jesus regularly invites others into his work of healing, teaching, and restoring.

This collaborative vision also honors the diversity and agency of creation. Human beings are not the only creatures with a role to play. Animals, ecosystems, social systems, and even natural processes contribute to the unfolding story of the world. God is present in all of it, luring each creature — according to its nature — toward beauty, wholeness, and relational harmony.

Of course, collaboration means the future is not guaranteed. What will occur is not scripted, fixed, or locked into a singular divine plan. This is a world marked by real openness, where love and creativity bring surprise, and where tragedy is a genuine risk. But God continually works to bring good out of whatever circumstances arise.

The collaborative world envisioned by open and relational theology affirms both divine initiative and creaturely responsibility. God is always active, always empowering, always present. We are invited to respond.

This view encourages a form of spirituality that is not about submission to fate or passively waiting for God to act. Instead, it cultivates attentiveness, participation, and co-creation. To live faithfully in a collaborative world is respond to divine invitations and to act courageously. It is to imagine our lives as part of God's ongoing work of creation, healing, and justice.

In such a world, theology becomes not just speculation about what God does, but a call to live in partnership with God. Whether through acts of compassion, public advocacy, scientific discovery, artistic expression, or everyday kindness, we join with God in shaping the world toward love. Every moment becomes an opportunity for collaboration. Every decision, a chance to say yes to God's loving lure.

Conclusion

Open and relational theology offers a fresh and transformative vision of how God and creation interact—a vision centered on freedom, love, and collaboration. Rather than depicting God as a distant ruler or cosmic puppet master, this theology presents God as a loving partner, working persistently and noncoercively in every moment to bring about the greatest good.

Human freedom is not an illusion. It is a gift that makes love possible and relationship real. With that freedom comes risk—of harm, injustice, and suffering—but also the opportunity for profound creativity, moral beauty, and authentic transformation.

Divine action, likewise, is not about imposing outcomes or violating agency. It is the subtle yet powerful presence of persistent love—inspiring, guiding, healing, and redeeming. In a world that is not fixed but open, God does not work alone. We are called into a collaborative life. God empowers us to participate—to help bring about a world marked by justice, compassion, and love.

Chapter 6
Love and Salvation

At the heart of open and relational theology is the conviction that God is love, and that every aspect of God's interaction with creation—including salvation—flows from this love. Rather than viewing salvation as a divine rescue plan predetermined before creation, open and relational theology understands salvation as a relational and ongoing process, grounded in God's unchanging commitment to seek the well-being of all.

This chapter reimagines salvation not as a transaction, a punishment-avoidance scheme, or a one-time decision. It points to salvation as a lifelong and communal journey of transformation. The chapter explores how love shapes the meaning of salvation, the role of human freedom and participation, and the expansive scope of God's redemptive work.

Salvation as Relational Healing

In many traditional models, salvation is primarily legal or forensic. Humanity is seen as guilty, and salvation means having that guilt removed through a sacrificial transaction. In many cases, this removal comes from Jesus' death as a substitute. While this model has had historical influence, open and relational theology shifts the focus from guilt and appeasement to relationship and healing.

Salvation, in this view, is about the restoration of and ongoing right relationship — with God, with others, with oneself, and with creation. It is not just about going to heaven after death but about experiencing and participating in divine love here and now. The problem is not merely legal guilt but relational alienation, woundedness, and distortion of love. Salvation starts now.

The biblical witness supports this vision. Jesus describes his mission in relational and restorative terms: "I came that they may have life, and have it abundantly" (John 10:10). He heals the sick, welcomes the outcast, forgives sins, and reconciles communities. Paul uses rich metaphors of reconciliation, new creation, and participation in Christ. In each case, salvation is portrayed as God's loving initiative to bring wholeness, not to satisfy divine wrath or fulfill a legal requirement.

In this light, salvation is not about escaping punishment but about enjoying a life of flourishing defined by love, compassion, and mutuality. It is relational healing, not legal correction. It is transformation, not transaction. And this salvation is not just for the individual or even the community but for all creation. God really loves the *whole* world.

Love That Saves Without Coercing

If God's nature is uncontrolling love, then salvation must also be consistent with that love. This means that God does not save by force. God invites, persuades, and empowers—but never controls. Salvation is, therefore, always a free, relational process, not a mechanical or magical event. And creatures always play a role.

God desires the salvation of all (1 Timothy 2:4). But in an open and relational framework, this desire is not automatically fulfilled. God lovingly calls every person into relationship, offering healing, grace, and transformation at every moment. But the human response remains essential. Love cannot be one-sided; it must be received and reciprocated to become mutual relationship. And creatures can choose not to cooperate with God's salvific love.

This view highlights the partnership between divine grace and human freedom. Grace is never absent—God is always working for our good—but love does not override our agency. We are invited to say yes, to participate, to cooperate in the ongoing process of salvation.

This is why Scripture speaks of salvation in multiple tenses: we have been saved, we are being saved, and we will be saved. It is not merely a moment; it is a journey. The ongoing work of salvation involves a myriad of moments. God acts and creatures respond.

Importantly, this view does not reduce salvation to human effort. It requires God's work—initiated, empowered, and sustained by divine love. But it also takes our response seriously. We are not passive recipients but active participants in our own transformation.

Because must be active participants in transformation, salvation is not God's work alone. The goals God has for universal salvation require positive creaturely cooperation. In this divine-creature synergy, flourishing can arise for individuals, community, and all creation.

The Life, Death, and Resurrection of Jesus

Most Christian open and relational thinkers believe Jesus of Nazareth is the clearest revelation of God's loving and saving nature. His life embodies divine compassion, his death reveals the costliness of love, and his resurrection proclaims the victory of life over violence and despair. In the ways, work, and wisdom of Jesus, we find salvation.

The cross is not a payment extracted by a wrathful God. Instead, the cross is a revelation of divine solidarity and suffering love. Jesus does not die to change God's mind about us, but his death at the hands of the Roman empire and supported by religious authorities reveal God's heart to us. The crucifixion exposes the depth of divine empathy and the lengths to which God will go to be with us, even in death.

The resurrection is not a proof of divinity or a supernatural triumph. God raised Jesus from the dead as a transformation of relationship. The raising of Jesus is the vindication of love over the powers of violence, injustice, and death. It is God's yes to Jesus' way of love. Salvation, then, is not just what Jesus does for us, but what Jesus invites us into—a life patterned after his own: humble, courageous, compassionate, and open to transformation.

The salvation God provides find its model in Jesus. But salvation is not just restricted to those who consciously follow this Nazarene. God offers salvation to all, no matter their religion or location. And when we respond to the call to love – no matter our religious beliefs or lack thereof – we find the salvation God desires for us.

Salvation as Ongoing, Communal, and Cosmic

Open and relational theology also emphasizes that salvation is not individualistic or escapist. It is ongoing, communal, and cosmic in scope. God wants the salvation of all, not just a few, not just humans.

Salvation is ongoing because it unfolds across a lifetime – and perhaps even beyond. It is not finished at conversion or baptism; it is the work of the Spirit in every act of healing, justice, forgiveness, and love.

Salvation is communal because we are not saved as isolated individuals. Because we are comprised of relations, our salvation must include the good of those with whom we are related. We are saved into community, into mutual belonging, into the body of Christ, where we learn how to love and be loved.

And salvation is cosmic. God's love is not limited to humanity alone. All of creation groans and longs for liberation (Romans 8:19-23). The redemptive work of God includes ecosystems, animals, institutions, and the physical cosmos itself. God's goal is not to evacuate souls from Earth but to renew the whole creation in love.

This expansive vision of salvation invites deep ecological care, social engagement, and spiritual humility. We do not know how or when God's purposes will be fully realized, but we live in hope, trusting that God's love never gives up and never runs out.

Prayer

In a world marked by freedom, unpredictability, and suffering, many people turn to prayer. Traditional theologies often present prayer as a way to align oneself with God's already-determined will or to plead for divine action in a cosmos God controls entirely. But in open and relational theology, prayer is neither futile nor merely symbolic—it is a real, relational interaction with a God who listens, responds, and is genuinely affected by our participation.

In open and relational theology, prayer is a meaningful, transformative relationship between God and creation. When we pray, we are not reciting words to a distant or unchangeable deity, but engaging with the living God, who listens, feels, and responds.

In contrast to deterministic theologies where everything is already foreordained and prayer cannot affect divine action, open and relational thinkers insist that prayer can make a real difference. God has not locked in the future. There are open possibilities. And because God is relational and lovingly responsive, our prayers can help shape what happens next.

In a world of genuine freedom and openness, our prayers provide God with new data, new desires, and new relational contexts in which to act. In this framework, prayer is relational participation in God's ongoing work of love in the world. Prayer creates new avenues for God's love to be expressed—not by overriding others, but by empowering cooperation, shaping circumstances, and inspiring action.

Open and relational theology suggests that prayer adds "relational conditions" to the world. This can enhance what God is able to do. Our prayers can open new paths—not because God lacked the will, but because divine love depends on cooperative relationships to achieve what unilateral control never could.

This view makes sense of unanswered prayer. If God does not control all outcomes, then God may not be able to bring about everything we request—especially when our desires involve the cooperation of others, or when they conflict with other goods in the web of creation. When prayers seem unanswered, God is still acting in the most loving ways possible given the circumstances.

This theology treats prayer as a real channel of cooperation between God and creation—one in which both partners contribute to the unfolding of new possibilities. And because God is always present, always listening, and always responding, prayer is not confined to set words or sacred spaces. It can happen in silence or song, in words or tears, in longing or gratitude. It is as wide as the human spirit and as specific as each moment. It is, at its best, a dynamic and participatory act of love, shaping both the pray-er and the world.

Conclusion

In open and relational theology, salvation is not a transaction but a relationship—a divine-human partnership rooted in uncontrolling love. It is a journey of healing and transformation, freely offered and lovingly received. It is the work of God-with-us, not just for us, drawing us into lives of grace, justice, and communion.

This vision moves beyond fear-based religion and into a hope-filled way of life. It invites us to live as those who are being saved every day—through mercy, through love, through connection with God and others. And it reminds us that salvation is not a finished product but an unfolding story, in which the God of relentless love continues to call, restore, and renew all things.

Chapter 7
Community, Church, and the Relational Body of Christ

Open and relational theology does not merely reimagine God — it reimagines how we live together in response to God. It challenges static, hierarchical, or institutionalized models of faith and community. In this framework, the church is not a fortress of certainty or a mediator of divine control. It is a community of becoming, grounded in love, shaped by mutuality, and called into the ongoing work of God in the world.

This chapter explores what it means to be the church in an open and relational universe. It considers how love, diversity, and participation are central to ecclesial life, and how the church can serve as a site of divine presence not through authority or uniformity, but through vulnerability, trust, and shared mission.

The Church as a Relational Community

In open and relational theology, the church is not first and foremost an institution, a building, or a set of doctrines. It is, at its core, a relational community — a dynamic and responsive gathering of people formed by love and called into mutual participation with God and one another. Rather than existing to manage spiritual transactions or defend theological borders, the church exists to embody divine love in ways that are concrete, contextual, and collaborative.

This vision emerges directly from the New Testament witness. In Paul's letters, the church is often described using the metaphor of a body (e.g., Romans 12; 1 Corinthians 12; Ephesians 4). This metaphor is not abstract: it emphasizes interdependence, diversity of function, mutual care, and unity through difference. "The eye cannot say to the hand, 'I don't need you,'" Paul writes, insisting that every member matters and that no part of the body can thrive in isolation (1 Cor. 12:21). Each believer is a unique contributor to the life of the whole, and the health of the body depends on the well-being of every member.

Because God is inherently relational — engaging with creation moment by moment in loving partnership — the community formed in response to God must also be relational at its core. The church is not merely a reflection of God's love; it is a participation in God's ongoing relational life. It becomes a living organism in which divine love takes shape through human interaction.

The early church, as described in Acts, reflects this ethos. After Pentecost, the believers "devoted themselves to the apostles' teaching and to fellowship, to the breaking of bread and to prayer" (Acts 2:42). They shared resources, broke down social barriers, and discerned their mission together. Their community life was animated not by uniformity or institutional control, but by a shared experience of divine presence and relational commitment.

This framework also redefines how we understand church membership and belonging. Rather than being based on conformity or doctrinal agreement, belonging in a relational church is based on covenantal relationship — a shared commitment to love, justice, service, and growth. In many traditional settings, church is a place where people feel pressure to perform holiness or suppress struggle. But in a relational community, authenticity is a strength, not a liability. The Spirit does not require perfection to move — only openness and trust.

Participation Over Control

In many traditional ecclesial models, the church is structured around a theology of divine control, which is often mirrored in church leadership and governance. If God is believed to singlehandedly decide outcomes, then those in ecclesial authority may see themselves as agents of that divine control. This can lead to rigid hierarchies, centralized power, and a model of church life that prioritizes order, uniformity, and top-down decision-making.

Open and relational theology offers a different starting point. It begins with the conviction that God never controls, but always invites. God's power is persuasive rather than coercive, participatory rather than unilateral. If God governs through love rather than force, then the church—called to reflect God's character—must do the same.

In this framework, participation becomes the heart of ecclesial life. Decision-making is not the right of a few, but the responsibility of the community. Authority is grounded not in coercion but in relational credibility and mutual trust. Open and relational theology sees God's authority not as domination but as relational influence. Accordingly, the church is called to model leadership that listens, collaborates, and adapts.

Scripture supports this model. In Acts 15, the early church faces a theological crisis: should Gentile converts be required to follow Jewish law? The apostles don't impose a solution from above. Instead, they gather, discuss, and discern together, saying, "It seemed good to the Holy Spirit and to us…" (Acts 15:28). The decision emerges from dialogue and communal openness, not unilateral decree.

Jesus himself exemplifies participatory leadership. He consistently resists worldly models of authority. "The rulers of the Gentiles lord it over them," he says, "but it shall not be so among you" (Matthew 20:25–26). Instead, Jesus washes feet, touches the untouchable, and welcomes questions. He empowers his disciples and entrusts them with meaningful work—even when they are far from perfect.

Open and relational theology follows this path by envisioning the church as a network of co-creators rather than a chain of command. This vision reshapes how we think about church governance and ecclesial structures. Committees, boards, councils, and congregational meetings are spaces for shared discernment. The messy, slow work of collaboration is not a failure of leadership but a sign that the Spirit is at work in the midst of human diversity.

In many churches, a small number of people speak, teach, lead worship, and offer theological reflection. But in an open and relational church, every voice matters. The Spirit is not confined to clergy or experts. God speaks through children, artists, skeptics, the wounded, and the quiet. Real spiritual authority arises not from control, but from the capacity to love, serve, and empower others.

This participatory model also affirms that the church is always in process. It is not a finished institution guarding eternal truths, but a living, learning body engaged in ongoing discernment. Because God is responsive, and the world is dynamic, the church must remain flexible and open to change. Doctrines may evolve, practices may shift, and new forms of ministry may emerge. The Spirit continues to call the church into new expressions of love.

Love, Diversity, and Becoming Together

At the heart of open and relational theology is the claim that God is love—not merely in sentiment or in abstract perfection, but in lived, dynamic relationship. Love is not static; it is creative, responsive, and endlessly generative. If the church is to reflect the character of God, then its defining feature must be love—not love as sentimentality or surface harmony, but as a robust, risk-taking, and co-suffering commitment to the flourishing of others.

Just as God's love is inherently relational and open-ended—inviting without coercing, empowering without dominating—the church is called to mirror that love in its structure, practice, and posture. And because real love does not seek to erase difference, the church must be a place that welcomes and celebrates diversity, not just tolerates it.

Open and relational theology affirms that diversity is not a threat to the church's unity—it is a witness to God's pluriform love. Thomas Jay Oord speaks of this love as *pluriform* because it takes many shapes, depending on the needs, contexts, and capacities of those involved. The church should expect to see the Spirit move in different ways through different people, cultures, traditions, and expressions. What binds the church together is not shared uniformity, but shared openness to God's ongoing work of love..

This diversity applies across every dimension: racial and ethnic identity, gender and sexuality, life experience, cultural expression, socioeconomic status, ability, and beyond. Love within diversity is not passive. It requires mutual vulnerability, active listening, and a commitment to justice. It resists tokenism and calls for solidarity. It means centering marginalized voices, repenting of exclusionary practices, and redistributing power.

Open and relational theology also reframes the church as a community of becoming. Rather than assuming a fixed identity or a completed theological system, the church is seen as a people always in process—learning, repenting, growing, adapting. Because the future is open and God is responsive, the church, too, is called to remain open to new possibilities and emerging expressions of faithfulness.

This idea of becoming together echoes the biblical narrative. The people of God are never presented as finished products. Abraham embarks on an unknown journey. Israel wrestles with covenant and identity. The early church navigates cultural conflict and theological expansion.

Spiritual formation, then, is not just about personal piety. It is a communal practice of becoming more attuned to God's loving call—in worship, in dialogue, in conflict, and in mission. The church becomes a kind of theological laboratory, where diverse people learn to live love together in real time. Mistakes are made. Forgiveness is practiced. And all of it is part of how the Spirit forms Christlike communities from a mosaic of imperfect individuals.

Ultimately, the open and relational church is a community that trusts in God's relentless, adaptable, and ever-present love. It is not a sanctuary from the world's complexity, but a sign of God's vision for relational wholeness amid that complexity. And in every act of mutual care, every conversation across difference, every shared moment of growth, the church becomes a living witness to what it means to love like God loves— relationally, diversely, and always becoming.

The Church in the World

In open and relational theology, the church is not set apart from the world in order to remain pure or untouched. It exists within the world and for the world—as a visible expression of God's loving presence and ongoing work in history. The church's mission is not to escape culture, nor to dominate it, but to partner with God in the healing, liberation, and renewal of creation.

In this light, the church's presence in the world becomes a practice of participation, not possession. Rather than claiming to hold exclusive access to truth or salvation, the church testifies to the character of God through its actions. Its vocation is to embody relational love—the same love that Jesus practiced in his table fellowship, healing ministries, teaching, and willingness to enter into suffering for the sake of others.

Jesus' own ministry offers the blueprint. He moves toward the marginalized, not the powerful. He calls attention to injustice. He tells stories that challenge norms and expand compassion. He breaks bread with outsiders. He heals not only individuals but restores them to community. In every act, he enacts the kingdom of God—not a distant place, but a reality breaking into the world through relational presence and justice-seeking love.

The open and relational church carries on that mission, recognizing that God's work unfolds in the flow of history through relationships, communities, and movements for wholeness.

Mission, then, is not about conquest but about cooperation with what God is already doing in the world. The church learns to recognize and join God's presence already there. Evangelism becomes invitation—not to a static belief system, but to a relational life of love and transformation

This cooperative understanding of mission frees the church from messianic pressure. It need not "save" the world—but it can be faithful to collaborate with the God who works moment by moment, through countless agents and unexpected means. Being "in the world" means engaging with the complexities of culture, science, politics, and art—not to baptize them uncritically, but to enter into dialogue, to learn, and to contribute meaningfully. The Spirit works through poets, protestors, scientists, and the unemployed. The relational church listens widely, knowing that truth emerges through unexpected partnerships and shared struggle.

In a world fractured by division, the church is called to be a reconciling presence. In a world driven by profit and competition, it is called to embody generosity and mutual care. In a world consumed by fear and despair, it is called to practice the kind of hope that trusts not in certainty, but in God's ongoing faithfulness. The church, then, is a community in process, becoming a people who live as if love is the deepest truth of the universe.

Conclusion

The open and relational church is a community in motion—a body not defined by boundary but by love. It is not a fortress of certainty, but a gathering of seekers, co-creators, and disciples. Its unity comes not from sameness but from shared commitment to the God who calls us into relational faithfulness and courageous love.

In such a church, everyone matters. Every voice contributes. It is a place where God's loving presence is not confined to sacraments or sermons but is found in conversations, meals shared, acts of justice, and prayers of hope. It is, at its best, the living body shaped not by control, but by love.

Chapter 8
Ethics, Justice, and Love in Action

Theology is never merely speculative. Open and relational theology calls forth an ethic of active responsibility rooted in love, freedom, and cooperation with God's ongoing work for justice. In contrast to deterministic or hierarchical moral systems that demand blind obedience to divine fiat, open and relational theology frames ethics as participation in love. The moral life is not about submission to an imposed code, but about growing into deeper relational awareness—with God, with others, with ourselves, and with creation.

This chapter explores how open and relational theology informs ethical discernment, the pursuit of justice, and embodied love.

Relational Responsibility

In open and relational theology, human beings are not isolated individuals nor puppets of divine control. We are free and relational agents, meaningfully embedded in a network of mutual influence. Our decisions truly matter—not just for ourselves, but for others and for God. Moral responsibility, then, is not about appeasing divine wrath or adhering to a universal formula, but about responding to the call of love in specific, evolving contexts.

Relational responsibility acknowledges that each ethical decision is situated in particular relationships—family systems, social structures, political realities, and ecological conditions. Every choice either fosters or diminishes the flourishing of those relationships. Because the future is open and situations are fluid, ethical discernment must be flexible, courageous, and attentive to the Spirit's guidance in the moment.

Most open and relational thinkers believer justice is part of love. After all, love is an active, embodied force that seeks the well-being of all, especially those who suffer under systems of harm and inequality. Justice, then, is love made structural, public, and prophetic. It is how love confronts injustice, restores dignity, and reorders the world toward flourishing.

The biblical witness is saturated with God's call for justice—not only as a personal ethic, but as a social imperative. The prophets denounce economic exploitation and political corruption. Isaiah decries "trampling on the poor" (Isaiah 3:15), Amos warns against "those who turn justice into bitterness" (Amos 5:7), and Micah calls God's people to "do justice, love mercy, and walk humbly" (Micah 6:8). Jesus continues this trajectory: proclaiming good news to the poor, release for the oppressed, and solidarity with those on the margins (Luke 4:18–19). The logic of love compels us not only to feel compassion but to actively oppose systems that diminish life and suppress agency.

Justice

Racial injustice is one of the most enduring and destructive relational failures in human history. It is not simply a matter of personal prejudice, but a systemic sin embedded in laws, economies, policing, theology, and cultural narratives. Open and relational theology insists that God is present in the midst of these injustices — not as one who endorses the but as one who suffers with the oppressed and calls for liberation.

This theology invites the church to stand in solidarity with communities of color, to name white supremacy as incompatible with divine love. Those who love must engage in the work of dismantling racial hierarchies wherever they appear — within institutions, neighborhoods, and the church itself. This includes amplifying marginalized voices, reexamining inherited theologies, and recognizing the relational wounds inflicted by racism.

Because God works in real time, moment by moment, justice work must also be relational and ongoing. It cannot be reduced to performative statements or episodic concern. It is a sustained participation in the Spirit's call to healing, repentance, and reparation — relationally and structurally.

Economic systems, too, shape the quality and dignity of human life. When wealth is hoarded, labor exploited, and basic needs commodified, relationships are distorted, and communities are fractured. Open and relational theology affirms that God is deeply concerned with economic justice—not because God prefers the poor in abstract, but because God's love always attends most urgently to those who are most vulnerable.

In this framework, God does not miraculously fix poverty, however, or redistribute wealth from on high. Rather, God invites communities to act in love and equity, inspiring reform. Churches are called to advocacy—speaking truth to economic systems and aligning themselves with workers, immigrants, and the economically marginalized.

Justice, in this light, is not an optional social add-on to spiritual life—it is a central expression of relational love. It is how we love our neighbors not only in feeling but in practice, in policy, and in power.

Love for the Earth

In open and relational theology, the scope of ethical concern is not limited to human relationships alone—it extends to all of creation. Our moral and spiritual lives must also include care for the earth and all its creatures. Climate change, environmental degradation, and the loss of biodiversity are relational and theological concerns that demand a loving, responsive, and justice-oriented response.

Relational theology affirms that the earth is not a disposable backdrop for human history, but a living partner in God's ongoing creative work. As

Scripture repeatedly affirms, the earth "belongs to the Lord" (Psalm 24:1), groans in longing for liberation (Romans 8:22), and reflects divine wisdom (Job 12:7-10). Creation is a beloved web of interdependence in which God is present and active.

From an open and relational perspective, God is not controlling the climate or punishing humanity through natural disasters. Nor is God likely to override human choices to "fix" the planet unilaterally. Rather, God is actively present within the systems of nature and the responses of communities—luring individuals, societies, scientists, artists, and activists toward solutions that promote ecological healing and long-term sustainability. This means that ecological ethics is not a niche concern—it is central to what it means to love well in an open and relational universe.

The open and relational model of uncontrolling love is especially relevant here. God cannot prevent environmental destruction without overriding the freedom of systems and agents, but God is always working to inspire and empower better ways of living. That includes calling people to reduce harm, shift cultural norms, develop renewable technologies, protect vulnerable species, and advocate for policy change.

Ecological responsibility, then, is a matter of loving participation in God's care for the world. It involves both personal and systemic action—reorienting our habits, economies, and values in ways that align with God's noncoercive, sustaining love. And in an open and relational universe, there is always hope, because God never gives up on creation. The future is still open, and the Spirit continues to inspire movements of ecological repentance, imagination, and resilience.

To love God is to love what God loves. And God loves this world—every river, forest, glacier, whale, coral reef, and grain of soil. To follow Christ in the 21st century is to take seriously the call to love and care for the earth as part of our deepest moral and spiritual vocation.

Discernment and Love as Embodied Praxis

In open and relational theology, ethical living is not about following a static rulebook handed down from on high. It is about discernment in relationship—a process of listening for God's call in the midst of real, evolving circumstances, and then responding with love.

This kind of discernment resists rigid legalism and abstract idealism. It acknowledges that ethical questions are often complex and situated. Instead of asking, "What is the correct answer once and for all?" relational ethics asks, "What is the most loving, healing, and just response in this particular moment, with these people, under these conditions?" The answer may change as relationships deepen, contexts shift, or new information emerges.

Love is the heart of an open and relational ethic. Thomas Jay Oord defines love as "acting intentionally, in response to God and others, to promote overall well-being." This deceptively simple definition affirms several key dimensions of relational discernment:

Intentionality means ethics is not reactive or automatic—it requires attention and moral imagination.

Responsiveness honors the dynamic interplay between persons, contexts, and God.

Overall well-being resists self-centeredness and narrow utilitarianism, calling us to consider the broad and lasting effects of our actions on people, communities, and the earth.

In a world marked by freedom and complexity, there may be no single "right" choice. Often, multiple good paths exist, each with risks and trade-offs. Discernment, then, is less about perfection and more about faithful responsiveness—seeking what love requires, acting in courage and trust, and being willing to revisit, revise, or repent as needed.

In open and relational theology, love is not a feeling we admire or an idea we contemplate. Love is a verb, a way of being in the world, grounded in attentiveness and enacted through concrete practices. Love shows up.

This kind of love is embodied, personal, and structural. It means caring for a neighbor and confronting the systems that harm them. It means sharing resources, forgiving enemies, feeding the hungry, and standing with the excluded. Love takes shape in protests and potlucks, in policy advocacy and pastoral care, in the daily work of parenting, mentoring, community building, and creation care.

Love is inherently hopeful—not because outcomes are guaranteed, but because God is always working with us to bring about good. When we fall short, God continues to work with what we've offered. The result is an ethic of love that is alive, resilient, and responsive. It calls us to be co-creators of good, not passive recipients of divine commands. It takes seriously the cost of love, while trusting in its enduring power to transform lives and systems.

Conclusion

In a world that is complex, uncertain, and often unjust, open and relational theology offers a compelling and hopeful ethical vision—one grounded in the ongoing, relational call of love. It affirms that every moment is morally significant, every relationship is sacred, and every human being is invited to participate in God's healing and liberating work in the world.

Because the future is open, ethics is not about submitting to a divine blueprint but about discerning, with God, the next most faithful step. Because God's power is noncoercive, we are not forced into goodness but are empowered to choose it. And because divine love is responsive and relentless, we are never alone in this work. God is always present—grieving with us, guiding us, and creatively working with our choices to bring about beauty, justice, and peace.

To live ethically in an open and relational world is to take up the vocation of love—not as sentiment, but as action. It is to listen attentively to the cries of the poor and the groans of the earth. It is to confront racism, inequality, and ecological destruction not with despair, but with hopeful, courageous participation. It is to believe that even in small acts of compassion, systems can shift, lives can be transformed, and new futures can be born.

Chapter 9
Hope, the Future, and the Unfinished Story

Hope is more than a feeling. It is a way of living, a theological stance, and a commitment to act—even in the face of uncertainty. In open and relational theology, hope is not rooted in the certainty of outcomes or a predetermined future. Our hope is the faithfulness of a God who never gives up working with us and creation.

This final chapter explores how open and relational theology reimagines Christian eschatology. Rather than a timeline of events or a scripted end, it offers a vision of the future as a collaborative, relational process—one marked by divine invitation, creaturely participation, and the continual outworking of love. Hope becomes an active, courageous trust in God's love, even when the future remains unknown.

The Open Future

In many theological traditions, the future is imagined as already known and determined by God. From this perspective, history unfolds according to a fixed divine script—one in which every event, from the smallest detail to the grand conclusion, is either caused or permitted by God for reasons ultimately aligned with a perfect plan. This view often aims to secure divine sovereignty, but it erases human responsibility.

Open and relational theology proposes a different vision: the future is not settled — it is open, not only for creation but also for God. God does not possess exhaustive foreknowledge of future free decisions, because those decisions do not exist to be known. Because the future is partly dependent on the real-time responses of free creatures and unfolding natural processes, the future is undetermined.

This openness redefines eschatology in terms of relational fidelity rather than control. God is the most responsive, resourceful, and loving agent in every moment — continually working to bring about the greatest possible good, given the circumstances. God works within the constraints of creaturely freedom and natural law to redeem and heal, without ever violating the integrity of creation.

This view finds strong support in Scripture. Biblical narratives consistently portray God as responsive and engaged in real time. God regrets (Genesis 6:6), changes plans in response to intercession (Exodus 32:14), negotiates outcomes (Genesis 18), and even seems surprised or grieved by events (Jeremiah 19:5; Hosea 11:8). Far from suggesting a fixed script, these stories present a relational God who adapts, responds, and feels.

This view encourages humility. We do not know what tomorrow will bring, and neither does God. But this is not cause for fear — it is the condition of authentic relationship. Rather than trusting in a fixed outcome, we are invited to trust in the God who walks with us, moment by moment, into the unknown future.

In this way, the open future is not just a metaphysical claim—it is a spiritual and ethical orientation. It calls us to live alertly, relationally, and responsibly. It opens up space for imagination, for risk, and for hope that is grounded in relationship with a God who is faithful, creative, and lovingly committed to the flourishing of all creation.

Hope Without Certainty

In many Christian traditions, hope is tied to eschatological certainty. The assumption is that God has already determined the course of history, and the believer's confidence lies in trusting a divine plan that will inevitably succeed. Heaven and hell are seen as fixed destinies. The Second Coming, the final judgment, and the new creation are scheduled events, known to God and waiting for their appointed time.

Open and relational theology takes a different approach—one that is less about certainty and guarantees and more about trust. Hope is not grounded in an unalterable script but in the character of God. Even in the midst of that uncertainty, we have hope because God is faithful, present, and always working for the good.

Thomas Jay Oord calls this divine faithfulness *relentless love*. It is love that never gives up, never ceases, and never fails to invite, empower, and seek the well-being of creation. In

Oord's words, *"God's love is inherently uncontrolling, yet relentlessly pursuing the good."* This provides a foundation for hope that is strong not because it eliminates risk or offers guarantees, but because it rest upon God's unwavering love.

Hope without certainty means we live in a world where things really can go wrong — and often do. Injustice persists, disasters occur, relationships break, and not all suffering is resolved in this life. But it also means that new possibilities are always emerging, and that God is never inactive or indifferent.

In the context of the afterlife, open and relational theology — especially as developed by Oord — resists traditional images of an eternal conscious torment. Instead, Oord suggests that *"if God's love is truly relentless and uncontrolling, then God continues to invite everyone — even after death — into deeper relationship, healing, and transformation."* Death does not mark the end of divine invitation.

This opens up a hopeful eschatology that is inclusive, ongoing, and redemptive. Rather than dividing humanity into the saved and the damned, the afterlife becomes a continuation of the divine-human relationship, still grounded in freedom and still open to growth. God never stops loving, never ceases to call, and never writes anyone off.

This hope challenges triumphalism and passive waiting. It invites active participation in God's redemptive work. If the future is open, then our actions matter. We hope with God for the healing of this world — and for the healing of all persons, even beyond death.

Resurrection, Redemption, and Our Role in God's Future

Central to the open and relational story is God's relentless work of redemption—a redemptive movement that includes not only individuals, but communities, cultures, ecosystems, and the cosmos itself. Within this movement, the themes of resurrection and human participation take on fresh meaning. They are not supernatural interruptions or divinely imposed conclusions; they are expressions of God's ongoing, persuasive love, working through and with creation toward renewal and wholeness.

The resurrection of Jesus stands as a central in open and relational Christian theologies. The resurrection is not a cosmic magic trick but a demonstration of God's fidelity to life, relationship, and restoration. In raising Jesus, God affirms that love is stronger than violence, that death is not the end of the story. New creation is already breaking into the world.

Yet resurrection is not limited to the past or to Jesus alone. It is the pattern of divine action in every age and context. Wherever love resists hate, wherever healing follows harm, wherever hope emerges from despair, resurrection is happening. In this sense, resurrection is not only an event—it is a way of life, a divine rhythm into which we are invited.

Cosmic redemption follows the same logic. Instead of anticipating the destruction of the world and its replacement with a pristine afterlife, open and relational theology envisions a renewed creation. The eschatological vision of Scripture — the "new heaven and new earth" in Revelation 21, the liberation of creation in Romans 8 — is not escapist fantasy but a theological promise: God will not abandon creation but continue working within it for its healing and fulfillment.

This is not guaranteed by divine fiat but pursued through divine fidelity. In a relational universe, even redemption is cooperative. God's desire to renew all things is constant and persuasive, but the fulfillment of that desire depends on creaturely participation — ours included.

This brings us to our role in God's future. If the future is not predetermined, and if God never works coercively, then the realization of divine purposes involves us. Our choices, actions, prayers, relationships, and communities all contribute to the shape of what comes next. We are not bystanders to eschatology — we are co-creators of it.

This does not mean that redemption is up to us alone. God's Spirit is always at work — luring, empowering, healing, correcting, and creatively responding to every moment of history. But divine action is relational. The kingdom of God is cultivated in and through lives that say yes to love.

This participatory eschatology also reshapes our understanding of vocation. To be human is not just to await salvation but to participate in the unfolding of God's dream for creation. Every act of compassion, every effort toward justice, every step toward reconciliation is part of how God's future arrives. Resurrection is not only something we hope for; it is something we help midwife.

And yet, we are not burdened with bringing about perfection. Open and relational theology does not rest its hope on human achievement. It rests on God's unwavering love—a love that continually works through our successes and failures, our courage and our limits, to bring forth beauty from ashes and life from death.

This means we can live with active hope and realistic humility. We can join God's work without assuming it all depends on us. The communities we form, the structures we build, the ecosystems we protect, the relationships we nurture—all of these are sites of divine-human collaboration.

To live in light of resurrection and cosmic redemption is to embrace a hopeful realism: that God is not done with the world, and neither are we. It is to believe that every act of love ripples forward and that nothing good is lost.

Conclusion

In open and relational theology, hope is not grounded in certainty, control, or a divinely scripted end. It is grounded in the unchanging, uncontrolling, and always faithful love of God. The future filled with promise because God remains lovingly present in every unfolding moment, persistently working for the greatest possible good with whatever creation offers.

We are invited to live as co-creators of a story that is still being written. This is not a hope of passive waiting but a hope that listens for the

Spirit's invitation, responds with courage, and joins in the labor of resurrection wherever new life is struggling to emerge.

This vision affirms that what we do matters. Our decisions, relationships, communities, and justice work—all of it plays a role in shaping what is yet to come. And yet we do not bear this responsibility alone. The God of relentless love walks with us, suffers with us, and empowers us to imagine and embody futures that reflect divine love.

And so we hope—not with naïve optimism or rigid forecasts. We hope with open hearts, active hands, and a fierce trust in the God who invites us to help build the world to come.

Conclusion
Living Open and Relational Lives

Throughout this book, we have explored the contours of open and relational theology. It's a vision of God and the world grounded in love, freedom, relationality, and hope. We've examined a God who experiences time moment by moment, who responds to creation, who does not control but lovingly invites, and who empowers us to participate in shaping a future that remains open.

This theology is not merely speculative. It touches every aspect of our lives—how we understand Scripture, how we pray, how we make ethical choices, how we confront suffering, how we view science, and how we build communities. It speaks to the deepest longings of the human heart: for love that listens, for freedom that matters, for justice that heals, and for a future that is not predetermined but filled with possibility.

Open and relational theology offers us a living faith for a dynamic world. It invites us into a relational journey with God, one marked by trust, creativity, humility, and courage. In this journey, we are not spectators to divine power but partners in a divine-creature dance.

To embrace open and relational theology is to embrace a life of deep responsibility and deeper hope. It means living as if love is the most powerful force in the universe—because it is. It means believing that what we do with our freedom matters to God, and that God never stops working with us, within us, and through us to bring about healing and wholeness.

In a time when many are disillusioned by rigid theologies, authoritarian systems, and visions of God that feel distant or detached, open and relational theology offers something different: a God who is profoundly loving, responsive, and persistently calling us toward greater something better.

This theology is not the end of the conversation. It is an invitation. An invitation to rethink. To reimagine what it means to be human in relationship with God, others, and creation. And most of all, it is an invitation to live—fully, freely, and faithfully—in response to the God who always love and never gives up.

May we become people who pray with hope, think with compassion, act with courage, and love without control. May we trust the God who is always near, always responsive, and always becoming with us. And may we co-create, with God and one another, a world more beautiful, just, and loving than we've yet imagined.

Appendix
More on Open and Relational Theology from Thomas Jay Oord

God Can't: How to Believe in God & Love after Tragedy, Abuse, and Other Evils (2019).

In this work, Oord challenges traditional views of God's power, arguing that God cannot prevent evil single-handedly. He presents a theology that emphasizes God's uncontrolling love, offering readers a framework to understand and respond to suffering.

Open and Relational Theology: An Introduction to Life-Changing Ideas (2021).

This book serves as a primer on open and relational theology, discussing key concepts such as God's openness to the future, relationality, and the implications of these ideas for personal and communal transformation.

The Uncontrolling Love of God: An Open and Relational Account of Providence (2015).

Oord explores the concept of providence, proposing that God's nature is inherently uncontrolling. He integrates insights from philosophy, science, and theology to present a model where God's love is non-coercive, which has implications for understanding miracles, evil, and human freedom.

The Death of Omnipotence and Birth of Amipotence (2023).

In this publication, Oord critiques the classical attribute of divine omnipotence and introduces the concept of "amipotence," suggesting that God's power is best understood as the power of love that empowers and nurtures rather than controls.

Pluriform Love: An Open and Relational Theology of Well-Being (2022).

Oord examines the multifaceted nature of love, proposing that understanding love in its various forms is essential to human and divine well-being. He discusses how this perspective influences ethical living and theological reflection.

God After Deconstruction (2024).

Co-authored with Tripp Fuller, this work addresses the challenges posed by deconstruction to traditional theology. The authors propose pathways for reconstructing faith that remain intellectually honest and spiritually fulfilling.

Questions and Answers for God Can't (2020).

This companion book to *God Can't* provides responses to common questions raised by readers engaging with the idea that God's love is uncontrolling. Oord addresses theological concerns, scriptural interpretation, and pastoral implications in a conversational format, making the ideas more accessible for study groups, classrooms, and individual reflection.

Creation Made Free: Open Theology Engaging Science (2009).

Edited by Oord, this volume explores how open theology interacts with scientific understandings of the universe, advocating for a view of creation that emphasizes freedom and openness.

The Bible Tells Me So: Reading the Bible as Scripture (2011).

Co-edited with Richard Thompson, this work addresses approaches to interpreting the Bible, emphasizing its role as sacred scripture in the life of the church.

God in an Open Universe: Science, Metaphysics, and Open Theism (2011).

Co-edited with William Hasker and Dean Zimmerman, this book delves into the philosophical and scientific implications of open theism, discussing how this view aligns with contemporary understandings of the universe.

Partnering with God: Exploring Collaboration in Open and Relational Theology (2021).

Co-edited with Tim Reddish, Bonnie Rambob, and Fran Stedman, this book discusses the collaborative nature of the divine-human relationship, emphasizing themes of partnership and co-creation in theology.

Defining Love: A Philosophical, Scientific, and Theological Engagement (2010).

Oord offers an interdisciplinary exploration of love, engaging with philosophical, scientific, and theological perspectives to provide a comprehensive definition and understanding of love's role in human experience and the divine nature.

Open and Relational Leadership: Leading with Love (2020).

Co-edited with Sheri D. Kling and Roland Hearn, this book explores leadership through the lens of open and relational theology. It emphasizes leading with love, highlighting the importance of flexibility, collaboration, and responsiveness in leadership roles.

Love Does Not Control: Therapists, Psychologists, and Counselors Explore Uncontrolling Love (2023).

Co-edited with Annie L. DeRolf, Christy Gunter, John Loppnow, and Lon Marshall, this volume brings together essays from mental health professionals who examine the concept of uncontrolling love in therapeutic contexts. The contributors discuss how embracing a theology of uncontrolling love can inform and transform therapeutic practices.

Open and Relational Theology and its Social and Political Implications: Muslim and Christian Perspectives (2024).

Co-edited with Jonathan Foster, Manuel Schmid, and Mouhanad Khorchide, this book explores how open and relational theology can serve as a bridge between Muslim and Christian communities.

www.ingramcontent.com/pod-product-compliance
Lightning Source LLC
LaVergne TN
LVHW021404080426
835508LV00020B/2443